Spot the Differences
Frog or Toad?

by Jamie Rice

Ideas for Parents and Teachers

Bullfrog Books let children practice reading informational text at the earliest reading levels. Repetition, familiar words, and photo labels support early readers.

Before Reading

- Discuss the cover photo. What does it tell them?

- Look at the picture glossary together. Read and discuss the words.

Read the Book

- "Walk" through the book and look at the photos. Let the child ask questions. Point out the photo labels.

- Read the book to the child, or have him or her read independently.

After Reading

- Prompt the child to think more. Ask: What did you know about frogs and toads before reading this book? What more would you like to learn?

Bullfrog Books are published by Jump!
5357 Penn Avenue South
Minneapolis, MN 55419
www.jumplibrary.com

Library of Congress Cataloging-in-Publication Data

Names: Rice, Jamie, author.
Title: Frog or toad? / by Jamie Rice.
Description: Bullfrog books.
Minneapolis, MN: Jump!, Inc., [2022]
Series: Spot the differences
Includes index. | Audience: Ages 5–8
Identifiers: LCCN 2021028400 (print)
LCCN 2021028401 (ebook)
ISBN 9781636903460 (hardcover)
ISBN 9781636903477 (paperback)
ISBN 9781636903484 (ebook)
Subjects: LCSH: Frogs—Juvenile literature.
Toads—Juvenile literature.
Classification: LCC QL668.E2 R525 2022 (print)
LCC QL668.E2 (ebook)
DDC 597.8/9—dc23
LC record available at https://lccn.loc.gov/2021028400
LC ebook record available at https://lccn.loc.gov/2021028401

Editor: Jenna Gleisner
Designer: Michelle Sonnek

Photo Credits: Fablok/Shutterstock, cover (left); Alexander Sviridov/Shutterstock, cover (right); Michiel de Wit/Shutterstock, 1, 20, 21; JGade/Shutterstock, 3, 14–15; Ilias Strachinis/Shutterstock, 4; Breck P. Kent/Shutterstock, 5; davemhuntphotography/Shutterstock, 6–7 (top), 8–9, 23tl, 23bl; Marek R. Swadzba/Shutterstock, 6–7 (bottom); Manuel Findeis/Shutterstock, 10–11, 23tr; Steve Byland/Shutterstock, 12–13; colin robert varndell/Shutterstock, 16–17, 23br; Michael Durham/Minden Pictures/SuperStock, 18–19; topimages/Shutterstock, 22 (left); Mari.Toch/Shutterstock, 22 (right); Steve Bower/Shutterstock, 24 (top); S-F/Shutterstock, 24 (bottom).

Printed in China.

Table of Contents

A frog has big, round
eyes on top of its head.

A toad's eyes are on
the sides of its head.

Which is this?

How to Use This Book

In this book, you will see pictures
of both frogs and toads. Can you
tell which one is in each picture?

Hint: You can find the answers
if you flip the book upside down!

Hop! Hop!

This is a frog.

This is a toad.

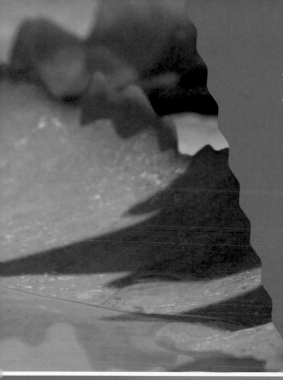

Both are amphibians.

They look alike.

But they are not
the same.

Can you spot the
differences?

A frog has smooth, wet skin.

A toad has bumpy, dry skin.

Which is this?

Answer: toad

skin

Frogs are often bright.
Toads are often dull.
Which is this?

Answer: frog

A frog's body is slim.

A toad is wide.

Which is this?

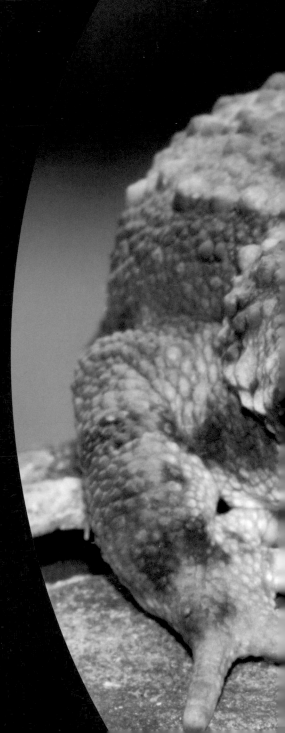

Answer: toad

A frog has big, round eyes on top of its head.

A toad's eyes are on the sides of its head.

Which is this?

A frog has webbed feet.

A toad does not.

Which is this?

Answer: frog

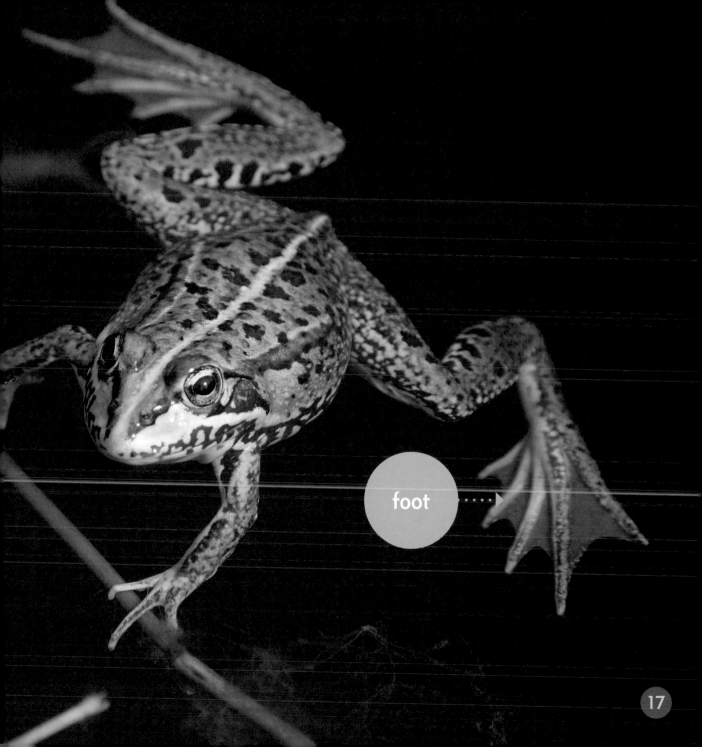

foot

A frog jumps far!
Its long legs help.
A toad has short legs.
It takes small hops.
Which is this?

See and Compare

Frog

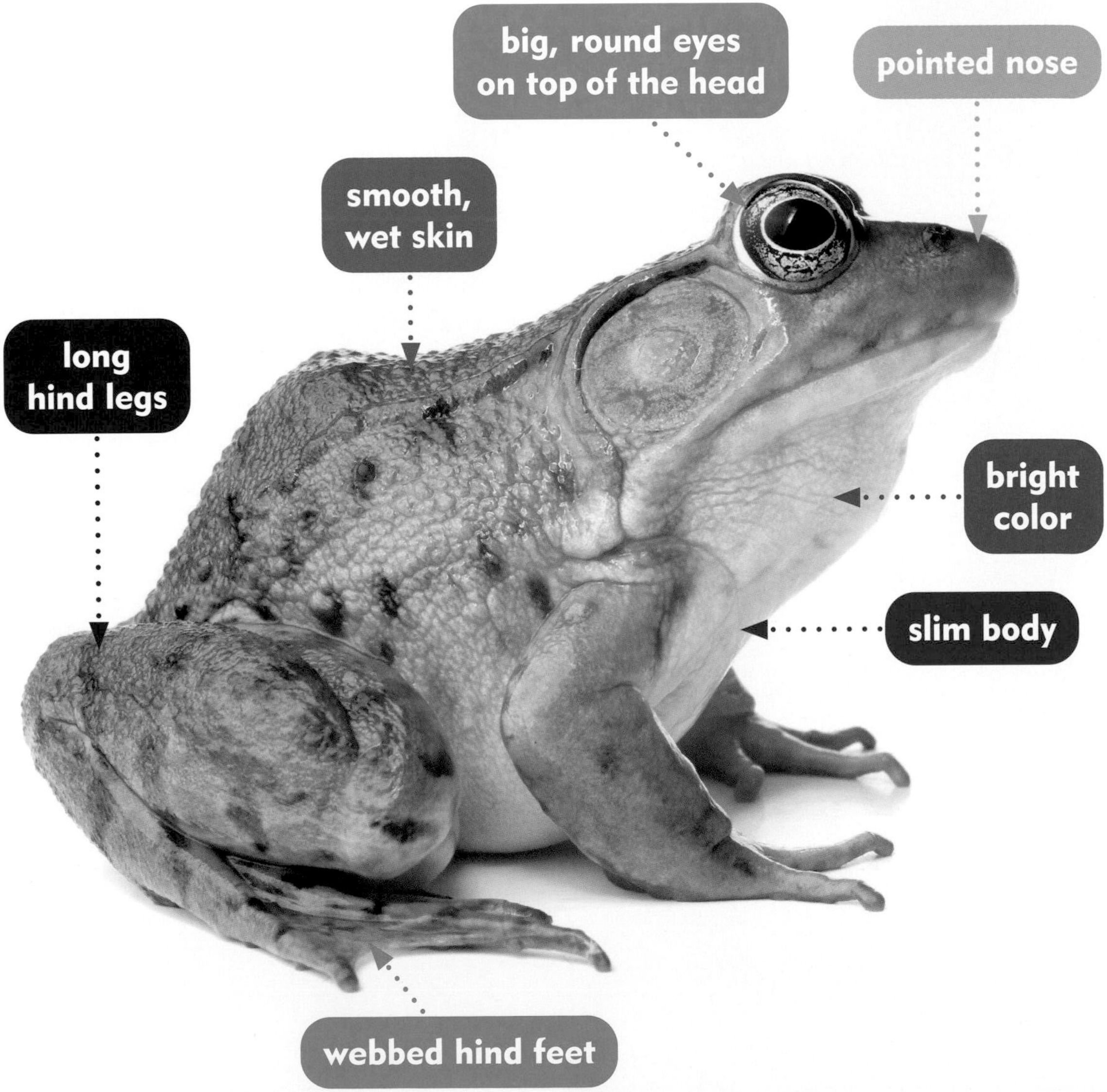

big, round eyes on top of the head

pointed nose

smooth, wet skin

long hind legs

bright color

slim body

webbed hind feet

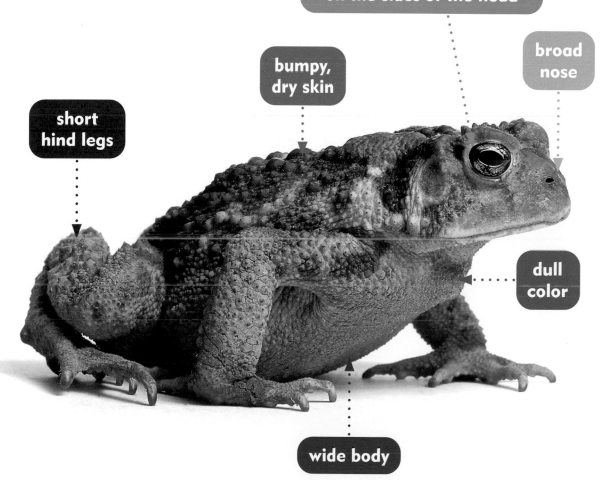

Toad

small, football-shaped eyes on the sides of the head

broad nose

bumpy, dry skin

short hind legs

dull color

wide body

21

Quick Facts

Frogs and toads are both amphibians. They are both born in water. As adults, they have four legs and can hop on land. They are similar, but they have differences. Take a look!

Frogs

- must live near water
- can live in trees or on the ground
- lay clumps of eggs in the water

Toads

- live in fields, woods, and gardens that are farther from water
- can only live on the ground
- lay strings of eggs in the water

Picture Glossary

amphibians
Cold-blooded animals that
live in water and breathe
with gills when young.

bright
Bold and vivid.

dull
Not bright.

webbed
Connected by a web
or fold of skin.

Index

To Learn More

Finding more information is as easy as 1, 2, 3.

❶ Go to www.factsurfer.com

❷ Enter "frogortoad?" into the search box.

❸ Choose your book to see a list of websites.

FACT SURFER